SCHOLASTIC
TRUE OR FALSE

Butterfly caterpillars

BY MELVIN AND GILDA BERGER

Front cover: Chushkin/iStock; Page 3: Scott W. Smith/Animals Animals; Page 4 & back cover: Richard Shiell/Animals Animals; Page 5: Robert Lubeck/Animals Animals; Page 6: Robert H. Armstrong/Animals Animals; Page 7: Millard H. Sharp/Photo Researchers, Inc.; Page 8: Arthur V. Evans/Animals Animals; Page 9: Maresa Pryor/Animals Animals; Page 10: Bruce Wellman/Animals Animals; Page 11 & back cover: James Robinson/Animals Animals; Page 12: Scott W. Smith/Animals Animals; Page 13: Naturfoto Honal/Corbis; Page 14: José Antonio Jimenez/Age Fotostock; Page 15: Bill Beatty/Animals Animals; Page 16: Perennou Nuridsany/Photo Researchers, Inc.; Page 17: Robert Maier/Animals Animals; Page 18: Skip Moody/Dembinsky Photo Associates; Page 19: Miller, Steven David/Animals Animals; Page 20: Phil Degginger/Animals Animals; Page 21: Maria Zorn/Animals Animals; Page 22: E. R. Degginger/Animals Animals; Page 23: Kevin Schafer/Peter Arnold, Inc.; Page 24: Scott W. Smith/Animals Animals; Page 25: BIOS/Peter Arnold, Inc.; Page 26: Patti Murray/Animals Animals; Page 27: Barbara Stmadova/Photo Researchers, Inc.; Page 28: Patti Murray/Animals Animals; Page 29: Gehlken, H./Peter Arnold, Inc.; Page 30: Hans Pfletschinger/Peter Arnold, Inc.; Page 31: Phyllis Greenberg/Animals Animals; Page 32: Patti Murray/Animals Animals; Page 33: Ken Thomas/Photo Researchers, Inc.; Page 34: M. Fogden/OSF/Animals Animals; Page 35: Dr. Jeremy Burgess/Photo Researchers, Inc.; Page 36: Donald Specker/Animals Animals; Page 37 & back cover: Gary Meszaros/Photo Researchers, Inc.; Page 38: Steve Gschmeissner/Photo Researchers, Inc.; Page 39: Kenneth H. Thomas/Photo Researchers, Inc.; Page 40: Patti Murray/Animals Animals; Page 41: Jeff Foott/Bruce Coleman USA; Page 42: Dwight Kuhn Photography; Pages 43—46: John P. Marechal/Bruce Coleman USA.

ISBN 13: 978-0-545-00392-6
ISBN 10: 0-545-00392-X

10 9 8 7 6 5 4 3 2   08 09 10 11 12

Printed in the U.S.A.   23
First printing, February 2008
Book design by Nancy Sabato

Butterflies have six legs.

TRUE OR FALSE?

TRUE! Butterflies are like all other insects.

They have three pairs of legs, which are attached to the body. Each leg is divided into four parts and ends in a tiny claw for gripping or holding on. All six legs are hinged to let the butterfly walk or land easily on leaves and flowers.

Butterflies have six legs, but usually land on only four.

Butterflies need the sun's warmth to fly or feed.

TRUE OR FALSE?

TRUE! Butterflies are sun-loving creatures.

They cannot warm themselves. They need the heat of the sun to warm their bodies for flying and eating. The flowers that butterflies feed on also need lots of sunshine. These flowers contain nectar—a liquid that is the butterfly's main food.

Butterflies rarely feed at night or in the shade.

Butterflies chew their food. **TRUE OR FALSE?**

FALSE! Butterflies don't bite or chew their food.

Their jaws are locked together at the bottom of the head to form a kind of feeding tube, called a proboscis (pro-BAHS-kiss). The proboscis works like a straw to suck up, or sip, the nectar from flowers.

Butterflies also sip water from puddles.

A butterfly will feed from any flower.

TRUE OR FALSE?

FALSE! Each kind of butterfly has its own favorite flower to feed on.

Monarch butterflies prefer milkweed. Painted lady butterflies usually choose thistles or zinnias. Other types of butterflies seek out marigolds, daisies, or crocuses.

There are many thousands of different kinds of butterflies— each with its own special flower!

Butterflies taste with their feet.

TRUE OR FALSE?

TRUE! The bottom of each butterfly leg has a pad with tiny hairs that taste the flower.

Many butterflies take only a few seconds to decide if the flower's nectar is good enough to eat. If it is, tiny claws at the end of each leg grip the flower. And the butterfly starts to feed.

Butterfly legs are weak, so these insects don't walk very far.

Butterflies have noses for smelling.

TRUE OR FALSE?

FALSE!

Most butterflies use their two long, thin feelers, or antennae (an-TEN-ee), for smelling.

The antennae grow between the butterfly's eyes. Each antenna has a knob at the end with sensors to pick up odors. A good sense of smell helps butterflies find food and mates.

Antennae give butterflies their sense of touch, as well as their sense of smell.

A butterfly sees what we see. TRUE OR FALSE?

FALSE! A butterfly doesn't see what we see.

It sees in almost every direction at the same time. That's because it has a large eye on each side of its head. And each eye is made up of many tiny, separate eyes. It also spots moving objects easily. Just try to creep up on a butterfly and see how fast it sees you and flies away.

Scientists believe that butterflies ca only see the colors r green, and yellow.

Butterflies have two pairs of wings.

TRUE OR FALSE?

TRUE! Like other flying insects, the butterfly has two pairs of wings.

It flaps all four wings at the same time when moving through the air. The larger the butterfly, the slower it beats its wings. A butterfly has to be careful that it doesn't tear or break its very delicate wings. A butterfly with damaged wings cannot fly.

Butterflies flap their wings four to twenty times a second.

Butterfly wings are covered with scales.

TRUE OR FALSE?

TRUE! Butterfly wings are covered with tiny, overlapping scales that are as fine as dust.

Under a microscope, the scales look like shingles on the roof of a house. All of the butterfly's color comes from its scales. Some scales have their own color. Other scales change color as the light strikes them.

Scales help keep butterflies warm by absorbing sunlight.

Butterflies
have few
enemies.
TRUE
OR
FALSE?

FALSE! Butterflies have many enemies—cats, birds, frogs, lizards, spiders, and humans.

To survive, many butterflies have strange designs, shapes, or patterns on their wings. A number have large spots, called eyespots, which can make the butterfly look like an owl or other animal. The eyespots startle the enemy, giving the butterfly time to escape.

A butterfly's eyespots may g bigger or small with the seaso

Some butterflies are nearly invisible.

TRUE OR FALSE?

TRUE! Some butterflies just blend into their surroundings.

This ability is called camouflage (KAM-uh-flaj). A few kinds of butterflies look like dead leaves. Some resemble the gray bark on trees or have wings that are bright on top and dull underneath. When in danger, they land on twigs or leaves and fold up their wings.

Some butterflies have see-through wings with very few scales, which make them nearly invisible.

The largest
butterfly in
the world lives
in the United
States.

TRUE
OR
FALSE?

FALSE! The world's largest butterfly lives in the treetops of New Guinea, far from North America.

The Queen Alexandra's birdwing has a wingspan of about one foot (30.5 centimeters). That's about the wing size, tip to tip, of a robin!

Laws now prote[ct] the endangered Q[ueen] Alexandra's birdw[ing] from hunters.

The smallest butterfly is the size of a thumbnail. TRUE OR FALSE?

TRUE! The world's smallest butterfly is the western pygmy blue.

Most of these butterflies live in tropical areas of Africa and the Hawaiian Islands. The pygmy blue, with its wings open, would fit on a dime. It is only a half inch (1.2 centimeters) wide!

Butterflies live in all continents around the world, except Antarctica.

Butterflies and moths look alike. **TRUE OR FALSE?**

TRUE! Butterflies and moths look alike, even though moths tend to be plump and fuzzy.

Another way to tell butterflies and moths apart is to see them at rest. Most butterflies at rest hold their wings straight up over their backs. Moths generally spread their wings flat over their backs.

Moths do not have knobs or bulbs at t' ends of their antenn like butterflies dc

Butterflies live only one day.

TRUE OR FALSE?

FALSE! Butterflies may live from two days to nearly a year.

Some hibernate, or spend the winter in a deep sleep. Monarch butterflies come together in large groups and migrate, or move, to warmer places for the winter.

Monarch butterflies migrate farther than any other butterfly.

Butterflies lay eggs in nests. TRUE OR FALSE?

Newborn caterpillars eat their own eggshells.

TRUE OR FALSE?

TRUE! The first thing the newborn eats is its own eggshell.

Each kind of butterfly lays eggs on a plant its young can eat. As each egg hatches, a small caterpillar crawls out. Then it starts nibbling leaves nonstop. A monarch caterpillar can finish a whole milkweed leaf in about four minutes!

A caterpillar never sees its mother—the female butterfly that laid the eggs.

Some caterpillars are blind. TRUE OR FALSE?

TRUE! A few kinds of caterpillars have no eyes.

But most caterpillars have six small eyes on each side of their head. Even so, they cannot see very well. Caterpillars can see the difference between light and dark, but they cannot see images.

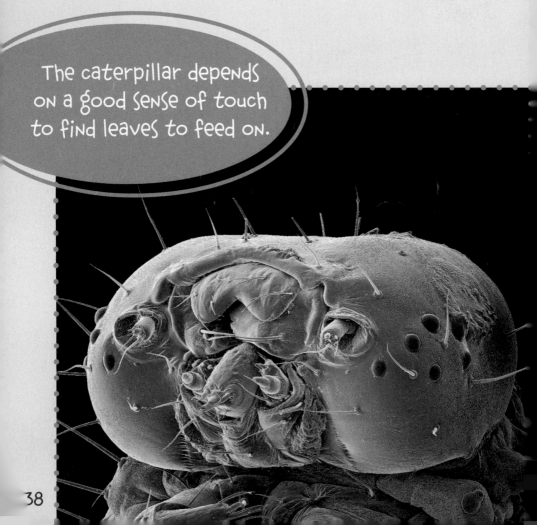

The caterpillar depends on a good sense of touch to find leaves to feed on.

caterpillars have no way to protect themselves. TRUE OR FALSE?

FALSE! caterpillars have a few means of defense against attack by birds and other enemies.

Some caterpillars look like bird droppings—and are left alone. Others have large eyespots on the head. This makes them look scary, like snakes, and the enemies flee.

Despite their defenses, most caterpillars are eaten by larger animals.

A caterpillar's skin does not grow bigger. **TRUE OR FALSE?**

TRUE! when the caterpillar gets too big for its skin, the skin splits down the back.

The caterpillar crawls out. Underneath, there is a new skin. Shedding old skin so that a new skin can grow is called molting.

Most caterpillars molt four or five tim as they grow.

A full-grown caterpillar builds a shell round itself. TRUE OR FALSE?

TRUE! when it is finished growing, the caterpillar hangs down from a twig or leaf.

It forms a hard, outer case called a chrysalis (KRIS-uh-liss) around itself. The caterpillar is now known as a pupa (PYOO-puh). Inside the chrysalis, the pupa slowly changes into a butterfly!

The change from caterpillar to butterfly is called metamorphosis (met-uh-MOR-fuh-siss).

Every butterfly has the same life cycle.

TRUE OR FALSE?

TRUE!

Each butterfly goes through the same four stages in its lifetime. The butterfly starts out as an egg. In a little while, the egg hatches into a caterpillar. The caterpillar eats and grows until it becomes a pupa. Finally, the pupa slowly changes into a butterfly. Egg, caterpillar, pupa, and butterfly: The life cycle is complete.

The butterfly probably got its name because many butterflies have yellow wings, the color of butter.

INdex

FALSE! Butterflies lay eggs on leaves.

Each egg is very small and often looks like a tiny jelly bean. In one to two weeks, caterpillars (not butterflies) hatch from the eggs. The newborn caterpillars look like worms or small snakes. In time, these caterpillars grow up to be butterflies.

Some butterflies lay more than 1,000 eggs at a time.